D1134303

A FABULOUS GIFT

A FABULOUS GIFT

Inspirations on Silence and Solitude

Edited by

EILEEN CAMPBELL

Aquarian

An Imprint of HarperCollins*Publishers*

Aquarian
An Imprint of HarperCollinsPublishers
77–85 Fulham Palace Road
Hammersmith, London W6 8JB
1160 Battery Street
San Francisco, California 94111–1213

Published by Aquarian 1994

1 3 5 7 9 10 8 6 4 2

A catalogue record for this book
is available from the British Library

ISBN 1 85538 333 0

Printed in Great Britain by
Butler and Tanner Ltd, Frome, Somerset

... solitude ... a fabulous gift from the gods.

MAY SARTON

INTRODUCTION

Whilst for Shakespeare silence was 'the perfectest herald of joy', a twentieth-century writer, May Sarton, has described solitude as 'a fabulous gift'. Silence and solitude are so precious and so enormously beneficial to us that *A Fabulous Gift* seemed a fitting title for this anthology. Neither appear to be easily available in our modern world. 'The world is too much with us,' to quote Wordsworth. All too often our lives, whether at work or play, are subjected to noise – telephones, computer hum, radios, chatter, traffic, machinery ... Our minds are constantly occupied too from the moment we wake up in the morning until the time we retire to bed.

Many of us find that we encounter silence and solitude when we are closest to nature. Throughout history there are many examples of those who have sought peace and tranquillity far removed from the distractions of the world. So the Desert Fathers went out into the wilderness, the ancient rishis of India retired from society, the Irish monks set out to sea in their curraghs. Hermits, saints and mystics have always known that silence and solitude are the greatest gift. So too have writers, composers, artists, philosophers such as Goethe, Mozart, Van Gogh and Descartes and scientists like Newton – to mention just a few. Then there are those who have thrived in enforced solitude. Boethius composed *The Consolation of Philosophy* in the sixth century whilst imprisoned in Pavia, John Bunyan wrote his spiritual autobiography in prison and possibly much of *Pilgrim's Progress*. Gandhi, in the twentieth century, used his time in prison for study and prayer. Others have also experimented with silence and solitude: Thoreau who went to live for two years at Walden Pond, lone sailors like Chay Blyth, Thomas Merton who became a Trappist monk.

However much we long to be at peace, the contrary is also true. We resist silence and solitude. It is difficult to be alone with oneself for any length of time. We need companionship and stimulation. If we can see the inner restlessness from these two opposing drives, for what it is, and realize that we don't need to be where the action is, in some particular place or with some particular person, to fill the yawning emptiness, if we can still our minds through the practice of silence and solitude, then we are not alone. We attain C. S. Lewis's 'abyss of great silence when you can no longer hear the echo'. We are in touch with ourselves, we can let go of all our needs, we can be at peace, we can hear the inner voice and be alone with God.

Silence and solitude are restorative, and in the inner silence (regardless of our external surroundings), spiritual nourishment takes place and self-knowledge increases. Never should silence and solitude, however, be an escape from the world. We must return and play our part in the community. Interconnected and interdependent as we are with everything, after the pilgrimage of self-discovery, we must return to the world. Neither can we hang on to the state of inner silence, for it will evaporate. It is only to be found in a continual seeking.

Silence is the perfectest herald of joy

Your hearts know in silence
the secrets of the days and the nights.

KHALIL GIBRAN

The silence of a flower: a kind of silence which we continually evade, of which we find only the shadow in dreams.

LEWIS THOMPSON

I find it wholesome to be alone the greater part of the time. To be in company, even with the best, is soon wearisome and dissipating. I love to be alone. I never found the companion that was so companionable as solitude.

HENRY DAVID THOREAU

When from our better selves we have too long
Been parted by the hurrying world, and droop,
Sick of its business, of its pleasures tired,
How gracious, how benign, is Solitude.

WILLIAM WORDSWORTH
THE PRELUDE IV 354

O Solitude! If I must with thee dwell,

Let it not be among the jumbled heap

Of murky buildings ...

JOHN KEATS

Why does a virtuous man take delight in land-scapes? [Because] the din of the dusty world and the locked-in-ness of human habitations are what human nature habitually abhors; while on the contrary, haze, mist, and the haunting spirits of the mountains are what human nature seeks, and yet can rarely find.

KUO HSI

People talk about the silence of nature, but of course there is no such thing. What they mean is that *our* voices are still, *our* noises absent.

S U E   H A L P E R N

What do we want most to dwell near to? Not to many men surely, the depot, the post-office, the bar-room, the meeting-house, the school-house, the grocery, Beacon Hill, or the Five-Points, where men most congregate, but to the perennial source of our life, whence in all our experience we have found that to issue …

HENRY DAVID THOREAU

We shall never be safe in the market place
unless we are at home in the desert.

━━━

CARDINAL BASIL HUME

You ask why I make my home in
    the mountain forest,
and I smile, and am silent,
and even my soul remains quiet:
it lives in the other world
which no one owns.
The peach trees blossom.
The water flows.

LI PO

For the Great Spirit is everywhere; he hears whatever is in our minds and hearts, and it is not necessary to speak to Him in a loud voice.

BLACK ELK

Learn to be silent.
Let your quiet mind listen and absorb.

━━━━━

PYTHAGORAS

Sitting quietly, doing nothing,
Spring comes, and the grass
grows by itself.

ZENRIN POEM

Silence purifies. Those who are dedicated to silence must preserve in our over-busy world zones of purified air. We must struggle against the asphyxiation, which threatens the cities of our consumer society.... We live in a world mentally polluted by verbal intoxication. If dedication to silence did not exist, it would be necessary to invent it.

PIERRE LACONT

And silence, like a poultice, comes
To heal the blows of sound.

OLIVER WENDELL HOLMES

Silence is unceasing Eloquence.
It is the best language.

RAMANA MAHARSHI

Let us become silent that we may hear the whispers of the gods ... There is guidance for each of us, and by lowly listening we shall hear the right word.

RALPH WALDO EMERSON

Listen to the silence as it echoes around you,
Ancient spirits dance to it.

AMBER COVERDALE SUMRALL

We collect data, things, people, ideas, 'profound experiences', never penetrating any of them ... But there are other times. There are times when we stop. We sit still. We lose ourselves in a pile of leaves or its memory. We listen and breezes from a whole other world begin to whisper.

JAMES CARROLL

Close your eyes and you will see clearly
Cease to listen and you will hear the truth.

TAOIST POEM

Teach us to care and not to care
Teach us to sit still

T. S. ELIOT

Training began with children, who were taught to sit still and enjoy it. They were taught to use their organs of smell, to look where there was apparently nothing to see, and to listen intently when all seemingly was quiet. A child who cannot sit still is a half-developed child.

CHIEF STANDING BEAR

'If it were just a matter of playing football with the firmament, stirring up the ocean, turning back rivers, carrying away mountains, seizing the moon, moving the Pole-star or shifting a planet, I could manage it easily enough. Even if it were a question of my head being cut off and the brain removed or my belly being ripped open and my heart cut out ... I would take on the job at once,' said Monkey. 'But if it comes to sitting still and meditating, I am bound to come off badly. It's quite against my nature to sit still.'

WU CH'ÊNG-EN (MONKEY)

Silence is the garden of meditation.

IBN ABÛ TÂLIB 'ALI

He (the American Indian) believes profoundly in silence – the sign of a perfect equilibrium. Silence is the absolute poise or balance of body, mind and spirit. The man who preserves his selfhood ever calm and unshaken by the storms of existence – not a leaf as it were, astir on the trees; not a ripple upon the surface of a shining pool – his, in the mind of the unlettered sage, is the ideal attitude and conduct of life.

If you ask him: 'What is silence?' he will answer: 'It is the Great Mystery! The holy silence is this voice!'

OHIYESHA

(CHARLES ALEXANDER EASTMAN)

Solitude is resonant with a music as remote
and vivid as the tremor of the stars.

LEWIS THOMPSON

The thoughtful soul to solitude retires.

OMAR KHAYYAM

He who knows does not speak:
He who speaks does not know.

TAO TE CHING LXXXI

There is a time to keep silence and
a time to speak.

Ecclesiastes 3:7

The mark of solitude is silence, as speech is the mark of community. Silence and speech have the same inner correspondence and difference as do solitude and community. One does not exist without the other. Right speech comes out of silence, and right silence comes out of speech ...

DIETRICH BONHOEFFER

Silence is the language of God: it is also the language of the heart.

SWAMI SIVANANDA

It is easy in the world to live after the world's opinions; it is easy in solitude to live after our own; but the Great Man is he who in the midst of the crowd keeps with perfect sweetness the independence of solitude.

RALPH WALDO EMERSON

You must have a room or a certain
hour of the day ...

JOSEPH CAMPBELL

All men's miseries derive from not being able
to sit quiet in a room alone.

BLAISE PASCAL

In thy chamber thou shalt find what abroad thou shalt too often lose.

THOMAS À KEMPIS

In solitude alone can be known true freedom.

MICHAEL DE MONTAIGNE

Most people want solitude because they want
to discover their unconditioned freedom,
where they are free of all definitions.

WILLIAM IRWIN THOMPSON

Solitude is freedom. It's an anchor, an anchor in the void. You're anchored to nothing, and that's my definition of freedom.

━━━━

JOHN LILLY

If we can be perfectly quiet and perfectly still with no attempt to overcome, destroy, remove, or escape from any situation or condition, the flow to the Spirit will rush in and there will be freedom.

JOEL S. GOLDSMITH

The strong grows in solitude where the
weak withers away.

KHALIL GIBRAN

I am here alone for the first time in weeks, to take up my 'real' life again at last. That is what is strange – that friends, even passionate love, are not my real life unless there is time alone in which to explore and to discover what is happening or has happened. Without the interruptions, nourishing and maddening, this life would become arid. Yet I taste it fully only when I am alone here ...

MAY SARTON

I feel the same way about solitude as some people feel about the blessing of the church. It's the light of grace for me. Never do I close my door behind me without being conscious that I am carrying out an act of charity towards myself.

PETER HØEG

I surround myself with silence. The silence is within me, permeates my house, reaches beyond the surfaces of the outer walls and into the bordering woods. It is one silence, continuous from within me outward in all directions: above, beneath, forward, rearward, sideward. In the silence I listen, I watch, I sense, I attend, I observe. I require this silence. I search it out.

ALICE KOLLER

Solitude, though it may be silent as light, is, like light, the mightiest of agencies; for solitude is essential to man.

THOMAS DE QUINCEY

Privacy, ultimately, is a migration to solitude –
to that place where we are fundamentally by
ourselves … some measure of [privacy] is essential to our souls.

SUE HALPERN

As far as the search for solitude is concerned, we live in a negative atmosphere as invisible, as all-pervasive, and as enervating as high humidity on an August afternoon. The world today does not understand, in either man or woman, the need to be alone.

ANNE MORROW LINDBERGH

There is convincing evidence that the search for solitude is not a luxury but a biological need. Just as humans possess a herding instinct that keeps us close to others most of the time ... we also have a conflicting drive to seek out solitude. If the distance between ourselves and others becomes too great, we experience isolation and alienation, yet if the proximity to others becomes too close, we feel smothered and trapped.

JEFFREY KOTTLER

All who seek the roots of life dig in solitude for them.

C. H. A. BJERREGAARD

It appears, therefore, that some development of the capacity to be alone is necessary if the brain is to function at its best, and if the individual is to fulfil his highest potential. Human beings easily become alienated from their own deepest needs and feelings. Learning, thinking, innovation, and maintaining contact with one's own inner world are all facilitated by solitude.

ANTHONY STORR

Nothing will change the fact that I
cannot produce the least thing without
absolute solitude.

GOETHE

Solitude is as needful to the imagination as society is wholesome for the character.

JAMES RUSSELL LOWELL

You do not need to leave your room ... Remain sitting at your table and listen. Do not even listen, simply wait. Do not even wait, be quite still and solitary. The world will freely offer itself to you to be unmasked. It has no choice. It will roll in ecstasy at your feet.

FRANZ KAFKA

The best thinking has been done in solitude.
The worst has been done in turmoil.

THOMAS EDISON

The greater part of our lives is spent with our-selves, no matter where or with what other people we may live ... our imagination is the only companion chained to us for the whole of existence.

CHARLOTTE WOLFF

Talent is best nurtured in solitude.

GOETHE

When I am, as it were, completely myself, entirely alone, and of good cheer … it is on such occasions that ideas flow best and most abundantly.

MOZART

The creative person is constantly seeking to discover himself, to remodel his own identity, and to find meaning in the universe through what he creates. He finds this a valuable integrating process which, like meditation or prayer, has little to do with other people, but which has its own separate validity. His most significant moments are those in which he attains some new insight, or makes some new discovery; and these moments are chiefly, if not invariably, those in which he is alone.

ANTHONY STORR

The happiest of all lives is a busy solitude.

VOLTAIRE

Solitude means more than simply being alone. It is the condition necessary for the psyche to replenish itself.

JOHN R. O'NEIL

Certain springs are tapped only when we are alone. The artist knows he must be alone to create; the writer, to work out his thoughts; the musician, to compose; the saint, to pray. But [we] need solitude in order to find again the true essence of [ourselves]: that firm strand which will be the indispensable center of a whole web of human relationships.

ANNE MORROW LINDBERGH

When it comes to the important things one is always alone, and it may be that the virtue or possible insight I get from being so obviously alone much of the time is a way into the universal state of man. The way in which one handles this absolute aloneness is the way in which one grows up, the great psychic journey of everyman.

MAY SARTON

Each soul must meet the morning sun, the
new sweet earth, and the Great Silence alone!

OHIYESHA

(CHARLES ALEXANDER EASTMAN)

All of us are solitaries: we are born alone through the birth canal into the world and time, and we die alone. No one can enter our interior experience, or its continuum with the outer world we call community.

Solitude is the human condition, the universal vocation to be human. It is the willingness, with Love indwelling, to go to the heart of pain to find new life and share it with the world even though you may be separated from it physically. It is from this commitment to be focused through the narrow gate of solitude that self-emptying love is outpoured, and the heart of the community, the heart of its pain, is transformed into the heart of joy.

MAGGIE ROSS

Go to your bosom; Knock there, and ask your
heart what it doth know.

Shakespeare
measure for measure II.II.136

Make your ego porous. Will is of little importance, complaining is nothing, fame is
nothing. Openness, patience, receptivity,
solitude is everything.

The capacity to be alone becomes linked with self-discovery and self-realization; with becoming aware of one's deepest needs, feelings, and impulses.

ANTHONY STORR

Solitude is the willingness to penetrate
illusion at any price.

MAGGIE ROSS

All men's misfortunes spring from their
hatred of being alone.

JEAN DE LA BRUYÈRE

Have the courage to be alone ... for once try to endure your own company for a while ... Don't speak, then, not even with yourself nor with the others with whom we dispute even when they are not there. Wait. Listen ... Endure yourself!

K. RAHNER

Solitude is a way of being with oneself, of learning to endure oneself, of becoming comfortable with the mystery that is one's Self. Solitude is a decision to encounter one's inner Self, and only decision allows it to become part of one's lifestyle.

OLIVER MORGAN

Everyone is really alone. That is why people crowd together. But in the full current of life there is no loneliness ...

Everyone is alone before God. One cannot really run away from God to any human being, lover or friend or child. Every soul in God says to every other: I am with you to the end of the world.

LEWIS THOMPSON

They are never alone that are accompanied
with noble thoughts.

PHILIP SIDNEY

For the most part, it is better to go with the crowd and be considered ordinary than to be endowed with a world of wisdom and be alone. For this reason, at times the greatest knowledge is to know nothing, or to affect to know nothing. It has been said that even in paradise, it is not good to be alone, that too much aloneness saps the spirit. To live a balanced life, it is sensible to be admitted to the life-styles of many. Observing the mistakes of others is an easier learning experience than benefiting from your own, though both are necessary. In this world we have little choice but to live with others, though the dull and crass make up the majority. To live alone one must have within himself either much of God, or much of the jungle beast.

BALTASAR GRACIÁN

There is no doubt that solitude is a challenge and to maintain balance within it a precarious business. But I must not forget that, for me, being with people or even with one beloved person for any length of time without solitude is even worse. I lose my center. I feel dispersed, scattered, in pieces. I must have time alone in which to mull over any encounter, and to extract its juice, its essence, to understand what has really happened to me as a consequence of it.

MAY SARTON

The capacity to be comfortably alone flows from satisfying experiences of being with someone else. What's more, satisfying experiences of being with someone else fuel a continuing capacity to be alone, without feeling adrift or lonely.

STEPHANIE DOWRICK

Solitude always depends upon one's own attitude. If you are suspicious of others, and you don't have the correct attitude, then even if you remain with people, side by side, you still feel loneliness. But if your mental attitude makes you feel warm towards other people, and you have a very sincere motivation towards other people – if you truly care about other people's welfare and are concerned with their suffering, and you share as much as you can – now this is a real remedy for isolation or loneliness.

(TENZIN GYATSO)

FOURTEENTH DALAI LAMA

… a hermit must have a deep experience of communion with humanity. Without this, you cannot be a hermit, because you would only be lonely. You would not be really solitary. To be alone and to be cut off from others would make you very unhappy, but to be alone, and to be deeply united with others, in deep communion, that is a possibility for which many people long. That is what I call solitude – over and against loneliness.

BROTHER DAVID STEINDL-RAST

Our language has wisely sensed the two sides of being alone. It has created the word 'loneliness' to express the pain of being alone. And it has created the word 'solitude' to express the glory of being alone.

PAUL TILLICH

I began to see that loneliness is neither good nor bad, but a point of intense and timeless awareness of the Self, a beginning which initiates totally new sensitivities and awarenesses, and which results in bringing a person deeply in touch with his own existence and in touch with others in a fundamental sense.

CLARK E. MOUSTAKAS
LONELINESS

Whatever those unacquainted with it may think, solitude and utter loneliness are far from being devoid of charm. Words cannot convey the almost voluptuous sweetness of the feelings experienced .... Mind and senses develop their sensibility in this contemplative life made up of continual observations and reflections. Does one become a visionary or, rather, is it not that one has been blind until then?

ALEXANDRA DAVID-NEEL

Being solitary is being alone well: being alone luxuriously immersed in doings of your own choice, aware of the fullness of your own presence rather than of the absence of others. Because solitude is an achievement. It is your distinctive way of embodying the purposes you have chosen for your life, deciding on these rather than others after deliberately observing and reflecting on your own doings and inclinings, then committing yourself to them for precisely these reasons.

ALICE KOLLER

I have a great deal of company in my house; especially in the morning, when nobody calls. Let me suggest a few comparisons, that some one may convey an idea of my situation. I am no more lonely than the loon in the pond that laughs so loud, or than Walden Pond itself. What company has that lonely lake, I pray? And yet it has not the blue devils, but the blue angels in it, in the azure tint of its waters. The sun is alone, except in thick weather, when there sometimes appear to be two, but one is a mock sun. God is alone – but the devil, he is far from being alone; he sees a great deal of company; he is legion. I am no more lonely than a single mullein or dandelion in a pasture, or a bean leaf, or sorrel, or horsefly, or a bumble-bee. I am no more lonely than the Mill Brook, or a weathercock, or the north star, or the south wind, or an April shower, or a January thaw, or the first spider in a new house.

HENRY DAVID THOREAU

Silence is the richness of the soul,
loneliness is its poverty.

███████

M A Y   S A R T O N

Living life to the full comes when the ultimate concerns have been faced: death, freedom, isolation and meaninglessness. How we face or avoid those concerns has profound effects on the ways in which we experience intimacy and solitude, closeness and freedom, aware-ness of self and others.

STEPHANIE DOWRICK

Society depends for its existence on the inviolable personal solitude of its members. Society, to merit its name, must be made up not of numbers, or mechanical units, but of persons. To be a person implies responsibility and freedom, and both these imply a certain interior solitude, a sense of personal integrity, a sense of one's own reality and of one's ability to give himself to society – or to refuse that gift.

THOMAS MERTON

Sink in thyself! There ask what ails thee,
at that shrine!

━━━━━

MATTHEW ARNOLD

Those who seek the truth by means of intellect and learning only get further and further away from it. Not till your thoughts cease all their branching here and there, not till you abandon all thoughts of seeking for something, not till your mind is motionless as wood or stone, will you be on the right road to the Gate.

HUANG PO

If we have not quiet in our minds, outward comfort will do no more for us than a golden slipper on a gouty foot.

JOHN BUNYAN

You try being alone, without any form of distraction, and you will see how quickly you want to get away from yourself and forget what you are.

J. KRISHNAMURTI

We are so busy we hardly have time to look at the people we love, even in our own household, and to look at ourselves. Society is organized in a way that even when we have some leisure time, we don't know how to use it to get back in touch with ourselves. We have millions of ways to lose this precious time – we turn on the TV or pick up the telephone, or start the car and go somewhere. We are not used to being with ourselves, and we act as if we don't like ourselves and are trying to escape from ourselves.

THICH NHAT HANH

No answer eludes us if we turn to the source of all answers – the stillness within. Prayer accompanied by meditation will always provide the answers we need for the situations facing us ... How comforting to know that all answers are as close as our quiet moments.

EACH DAY A NEW BEGINNING

... only when we are silent can we begin to hear the voice that is truly our own – what the Quakers call 'the still small voice within' ... The source of this voice – which may be without sound, and yet is heard – is called by many different names: the inner guide, guardian angel, spirit guide, the collective unconscious, or just plain intuition. Actually all of us hear the whisperings of this voice every single day of our lives, but many ignore it.

RICK FIELD

Every moment there is news coming
out of silence.

RAINER MARIA RILKE

Each of us will hear a different voice, one that is unique to us, and we will each be called in a different direction. But once heard, we must find the courage to reunite with that voice and trust where it leads. It is the voice of our truest nature. If we fail to hear its inner call, we will be less than we might have been, and we will never truly find peace and a sense of completeness.

MARILYN BARRETT

Like water which can clearly mirror the sky and the trees only so long as its surface is undisturbed, the mind can only reflect the true image of the Self when it is tranquil and wholly relaxed.

INDRA DEVI

To a mind that is still
The whole universe surrenders

CHUANG TZU

Mind is like a candle flame: unstable, flickering, constantly changing, fanned by the violent winds of our thoughts and emotions. The flame will only burn steadily when we can calm the air around it; so we can only begin to glimpse and rest in the nature of mind when we have stilled the turbulence of our thoughts and emotions.

SOGYAL RINPOCHE

The poor long for riches and the rich for heaven, but the wise long for a state of tranquillity.

S W A M I   R A M A

Listen in deep silence.
Be very still and open your mind ...
Sink deep into the peace that waits for you
beyond the frantic, riotous thoughts
and sights and sounds of this insane world.

A Course in Miracles

Contradictions have always existed in the soul of man. But it is only when we prefer analysis to silence that they become a constant and insoluble problem. We are not meant to resolve all contradictions but to live with them and rise above them and see them in the light of exterior and objective values which make them trivial by comparison.

THOMAS MERTON

We do not need any deep metaphysics: we need to understand the simple little truth that the still small Voice is the power that destroys the illusions of this world.

JOEL S. GOLDSMITH

Oh God, make us children of quietness, and heirs of peace.

ST CLEMENT OF ALEXANDRIA

Whatever, by limiting you to some level of surface response, hides your solitude, hides the truth: you are hidden from yourself, cut off from the springs of your existence, reduced to a blind marionette.

LEWIS THOMPSON

[Solitude] has to be a communion in something greater than the world, as great as Being itself, in order that in its deep peace we may find God.

THOMAS MERTON

For thus said the Lord God, the Holy one
  of Israel:
In returning and rest you shall be saved;
In quietness and in trust shall be your strength.

ISAIAH 30:15

Rest in natural great peace

This exhausted mind

Beaten helpless by karma and neurotic
    thought,

Like the relentless fury of the pounding waves

In the infinite ocean of samsara.

NYOSHUL KHENPO

O Krishna, the mind is restless, turbulent,
strong and unyielding; I consider it as difficult
to subdue as the wind.

BHAGAVAD-GITA VI.34

Mind is filled with various impressions, passions, and thoughts. All these should be emptied from the mind .... Moral discipline is [practised] to create peace in the mind. Without peace, prosperity becomes meaningless. Meditation on God becomes impossible when there is no peace in the mind. When any desire remains, meditation is not possible. One's soul concern in life should be God-realization. Life should become secondary.

Shivapuri Baba

When man closes his lips, it is then that
God speaks.

HAZRAT INAYAT KHAN

One word spoke the Father, which Word was His Son, and this Word He speaks ever in eternal silence, and in silence must it be heard by the soul.

St John of the Cross

And behold, the Lord passed by, and a great and strong wind rent the mountains, and brake in pieces the rocks before the Lord; but the Lord was not in the wind. And after the wind an earthquake; but the Lord was not in the earthquake. And after the earthquake a fire; but the Lord was not in the fire. And after the fire a still small voice.

I KINGS 19:11–12

Breathe through the heats of our desire

Thy coolness and Thy balm;

Let sense be dumb, let flesh retire;

Speak through the earthquake, wind, and fire,

O still small voice of calm!

JOHN WHITTIER

How then are we going to reach God? How, but in quietness and in confidence, in the stillness and the Silence? How, but by learning to abide in a quietness within, by being still.

JOEL S. GOLDSMITH

The more he regards everything as divine ... the more God will be pleased with him. To be sure, this requires effort and love, a careful cultivation of the spiritual life, and a watchful, honest, active oversight of all one's mental attitudes toward things and people. It is not to be learned by world-flight, running away from things, turning solitary and going apart from the world. Rather one must learn an inner solitude, wherever or with whomsoever he may be. He must learn to penetrate things and find God there, to get a strong impression of God firmly fixed in his mind.

MEISTER ECKHART

That place which is everywhere at all times present (being the basis of all that evolves) and in which, in the beginning, at the end, or in the middle, there is no living creature, that place which is their own Self, the yogis call 'Solitude'.

TEJO-BINDU UPANISHAD 1.23

There is nothing so much like God in all the
universe as silence.

MEISTER ECKHART

As soon as He speaks my name, my silence is the silence of infinite life, and I know that I *am* because my heart has opened to my Father in the echo of the eternal years.

My life is a listening, His is a speaking. My salvation is to hear and respond. For this, my life must be silent. Hence, my silence is my salvation.

THOMAS MERTON

We have to learn to listen in different ways and in different places: in silence and in noise. Perhaps it is because so many paople have lost the art of listening that they have also lost the ability to pray.

SHEILA CASSIDY

'Be still and know that I am God.' Here 'stillness' is a total surrender without a vestige of individuality. Stillness will prevail and there will be no agitation of mind. Agitation of mind is the cause of desire, the sense of doership and personality. If that is stopped, there is quiet.

R A M A N A   M A H A R S H I

The more faithfully you listen to the voice within you, the better you will hear what is sounding outside. And only he who listens can speak.

DAG HAMMARSKJÖLD

When thou standest still from thinking and willing of self, the eternal hearing, seeing, and speaking will be revealed to thee, and so God heareth and seeth through thee. Thine own hearing, willing, and seeing hindereth thee, that thou dost not see nor hear God.

JACOB BOEHME

Deep in the soul, below pain, below all the distraction of life, is a silence vast and grand – an infinite ocean of calm, which nothing can disturb; Nature's own exceeding peace, which 'passes understanding'. That which we seek with passionate longing, here and there, upward and outward, we find at last within ourselves.

C.M.C. QUOTED IN R. M. BUCKE
COSMIC CONSCIOUSNESS

To preserve the silence within – amid all the noise. To remain open and quiet, a moist humus in the fertile darkness where the rain falls and the grain ripens – no matter how many tramp across the parade-ground in whirling dust under an arid sky.

DAG HAMMARSKJÖLD

Be still and know that I am God.

And so, for the first time in my life, perhaps, I took the lamp and, leaving the zone of everyday occupations and relationships where everything seems clear, I went down into my inmost self, to the deepest abyss whence I feel dimly that my power of action emanates. But as I moved further and further away from the conventional certainties by which social life is superficially illuminated, I became aware that I was losing contact with myself. At each step of the descent a new person was disclosed within me of whose name I was no longer sure, and who no longer obeyed me. And when I had to stop my exploration because the path faded from beneath my steps, I found a bottomless abyss at my feet, and out of it comes – arising I know not from where – the current which I dare to call My Life.

TEILHARD DE CHARDIN

So it is that every spiritual healing is the result of one individual sitting in the Silence, quietly, peacefully waiting, and then the Spirit comes through the consciousness of that one – the voice thunders in the Silence, and the earth melts.

JOEL S. GOLDSMITH

I was utterly alone with the sun and the earth.
Lying down on the grass, I spoke in my soul to
the earth, the sun, the air, and the distant sea ...

RICHARD JEFFERIES

Seek refuge in inner calm, free your thoughts
from the external world and you will feel the
rays of God's goodness and love pouring over
you and the universe.

IRANSCHAHR

There is a silence
into which the world cannot intrude.
There is an ancient peace
you carry in your heart
and have not lost.

A Course in Miracles

Praying is not about asking; it's about listening ... It is just opening your eyes to see what was there all along.

CHAGDUD TULKU RINPOCHE

... when thou art quiet and silent, then art thou as God was before nature and creature; thou art that which God then was; thou art that whereof he made thy nature and creature: Then thou hearest and seest even with that wherewith God himself saw and heard in thee, before ever thine own willing or thine own seeing began.

Daily silence experienced in humility and fervour as an indispensable exercise in spiritual nourishment gradually creates within us a permanent state of silence. The soul discovers in such silence unsuspected possibilities. It realizes that life can be lived at different levels.

PIERRE LACONT

Thou wilt keep him in perfect peace
whose mind is stayed on thee.

ISAIAH 26:3

Perfect bliss grows only in the heart
made tranquil.

HINDU PROVERB

Deep within, in the Heart of man,

there God has chosen his resting place;

there he finds his joy –

if only we would do that too;

perceive those depths that lie within,

And leaving all behind

retire to rest therein

– Yet no one ever does.

And even so it may often be,

That a man upon his daily round

be urged ten times, or more, to look within

– Yet still no one ever does.

JOHANNES TAULER

When man sits,
then the coarse passions subside
and the luminous mind
arises in awareness:
Thus consciousness is illuminated.

MEISTER ECKHART

Learn to love solitude, and, ever alert, think
of me without ceasing.

SRIMAD BHAGAVATAM

God will come to you much sooner,
if you will but stay completely still,
instead of searching for him wildly,
till body and soul fall ill.

▬

ANGELUS SILESIUS

Now consider what St Augustine said. He sought Him in many places and came to find Him within himself ... However quietly we may speak, He is so near that He well hear us ... a restless soul has no need of wings to go to seek Him, but only to place herself in solitude, to consider Him within her ... If you speak, try to remember that there is one within you to Whom you may speak; if you are listening, recollect that you have one to listen to, Who speaks more nearly ...

ST TERESA OF AVILA

I will sit
and be silent
and listen to
God's voice within me.

MEISTER ECKHART

As long as the soul is not still there can be no vision, but when stillness has brought us into the presence of God, then another sort of silence, much more absolute, intervenes: the silence of a soul that is not only still and recollected but which is overawed in an act of worship by God's presence.

METROPOLITAN ANTHONY BLOOM

When the soul collects all its interior powers within, and when the body collects all its external senses and unites them to the soul, the Holy Spirit approaches and breathes into this union quietude and peace …

FATHER ANDREW

The more we receive in silent prayer, the more we can give in our active life. We need silence in order to be able to touch souls. The essential thing is not what we say, but what God says to us and through us. All our words will be useless unless they come from within – words which do not give the light of Christ increase the darkness.

MALCOLM MUGGERIDGE

... silence and solitude invite me to a gradual letting go of all the outer voices that give me a sense of well-being among my fellow humans and to trust in the inner voice that reveals to me my true nature. Silence and solitude call me to detach myself from the scaffolding of daily life and to explore whether there is anything there that can stand on its own when the traditional support systems have been pulled away.

HENRI J. M. NOUWEN

There is a place in you
where there is perfect peace.
There is a place in you
where nothing is impossible.
There is a place in you
where the strength of God abides.

▬

A COURSE IN MIRACLES

Let him who cannot be alone beware of community. He will only do harm to himself and to the community. Alone you stood before God when He called you; alone you had to answer that call; alone you had to struggle and pray; and alone you will die and give an account to God. You cannot escape from yourself; for God has singled you out! If you refuse to be alone you are rejecting Christ's call to you, and you can have no part in the community of those who are called …

But the reverse is also true: Let him who is not in community beware of being alone. Into the community you were called, the call was not meant for you alone; in the community of the called you bear your cross, you struggle, you pray. You are not alone, even in death, and on the Last Day you will be only one member of the great congregation of Jesus Christ. If you scorn the fellowship of the brethren, you reject the call of Jesus Christ, and thus your solitude can only be hurtful to you.

DIETRICH BONHOEFFER

The hermit has an obligation to offer to the world what he has received as enlightenment in his isolation.

LAMBROS KAMPERIDES

There are really only two things to do: one is to be still and listen, the other is to take spiritually based action. Everything else is bogus activity which only gets in the way of your real understanding.

JOY HOUGHTON

For a full day and two nights I have been alone … And it seemed to me, separated from my own species, that I was nearer to others … I felt a kind of impersonal kinship with them and a joy in that kinship. Beauty of earth and sea and air meant more to me. I was in harmony with it, melted into the universe, lost in it, as one is lost in a canticle of praise, swelling from an unknown crowd in a cathedral. 'Praise ye the Lord, all ye fishes of the sea – all ye birds of the air – all ye children of men – Praise ye the Lord!'

Yes, I felt closer to my fellow men, too, even in my solitude. For it is not physical solitude that actually separates one from other men, not physical isolation, but spiritual isolation. It is not the desert island nor the stony wilderness that cuts you from the people you love. It is the wilderness in the mind, the desert wastes in the heart through which one wanders lost and a stranger. When one is a stranger to oneself then one is estranged from others, too. If one is out of touch with oneself, then one cannot touch others .... Only when one is connected to one's own core is one connected to others .... And for me, the core, the inner spring, can best be refound through silence.

ANNE MORROW LINDBERGH

We sense that there can be no true communion between human beings until they have in fact become beings: for to be able to give oneself one must have taken possession of oneself in that painful solitude outside of which nothing belongs to us and we have nothing to give ... And one might even say that I begin to communicate with others as soon as I begin to communicate with myself. So true it is that the most tragic solitude is that which keeps me from forcing the barrier between what I think I am from what I am: because then my consciousness has become such a stranger to my true self and my distress is so great that I can no longer say what I desire nor what I lack. Solitude is to feel the presence in oneself of a power that cannot act, but which, as soon as it is able to, obliges me to realize myself by multiplying my relation with myself and with all human beings.

Nevertheless this solitude into which we have just come, and which gives us such a strong sense of inner responsibility, and at the same time of the impossibility of being self-sufficient, is experienced as a solitude only because it is at the same time an appeal toward solitudes like our own with whom we feel the need to be in communion; for it is only through this communion that each consciousness will discover the essence of its destiny which is not to perceive things or to dominate them, but is to live, and that means to find outside itself other consciousnesses from which it never stops receiving and to whom it never stops giving in an uninterrupted circuit of light, of joy and of love, which is the only law of the spiritual universe.

LOUIS LAVELLE QUOTED IN

MAY SARTON

… it is clear that we are usually surrounded by so much outer noise that it is hard to truly hear our God when he is speaking to us. We have often become deaf, unable to know when God calls us and unable to understand in which direction he calls us.

Thus our lives become absurd. In the word *absurd* we find the Latin word *surdus*, which means 'deaf'. A spiritual life requires discipline because we need to learn to listen to God, who constantly speaks but whom we seldom hear.

When, however, we learn to listen, our lives become obedient lives. The word *obedient* comes from the Latin word *audire*, which means 'listening'. A spiritual discipline is necessary in order to move slowly from an absurd to an obedient life, from a life in which there is some free inner space when we can listen to our God and follow his guidance.

Jesus' life was a life of obedience. He was always listening to the Father, always attentive to his voice, always alert for his directions. Jesus was 'all ear'. That is true prayer: being all ear for God. The core of all prayer is indeed listening, obediently standing in the presence of God.

HENRI J. M. NOUWEN

Solitude is one of the deepest disciplines of the spiritual life because it crucifies our need for importance and prominance.

Everyone – including ourselves at first – will see our solitude as a waste of good time. We are removed from 'where the action is'. That, of course, is exactly what we need. In silence and solitude God slowly but surely frees us from our egomania.

In time we come to see that the really important action occurs in solitude. Once we have experienced God at work in the soul, all the blare and attention of the world seem like a distant and fragmentary echo. Only then are we able to enter the hustle and bustle of today's machine civilization with perspective and freedom.

RICHARD J. FOSTER

ACKNOWLEDGEMENTS AND FURTHER READING

The editor would like to thank the following authors and publishers for permission to reprint material from their books:

Bloom, Metropolitan Anthony, *Living Prayer* (DLT).

Boehme, Jacob, *The Signature of All Things and Other Writings* (James Clarke, 1969).

Bonhoeffer, Dietrich, *Life Together* (SCM Press).

Cassidy, Sheila, *Prayer for Pilgrims* (Fount, 1980).

Cooper, David A., *Simplicity and Solitude: A Guide for Spiritual Retreat* (Bell Tower, 1992).

Dillard, Annie, *Pilgrim at Tinker Creek* (Picador, 1976).

Dowrick, Stephanie, *Intimacy and Solitude: Balancing Closeness and Independence* (The Women's Press, 1992).

Emerson, Ralph Waldo, *Society and Solitude in the Works of Ralph Waldo Emerson* (Nimmo, Hay & Mitchell, 1906).

Father Andrew, *In the Silence* (A. R. Mowbray).

Field, Rick, *Chop Wood, Carry Water*

Foster, Richard and Smith, James Bryan (eds), *Devotional Classics* (Hodder & Stoughton, 1990).

Gibran, Khalil, *The Prophet* (copyright 1923, Khalil Gibran; renewal copyright, 1951, Knopf, New York, William Heinemann, 1926).

Goldsmith, Joel S., *The Thunder of Silence* (HarperCollins, 1961).

Halpern, Sue, *Migrations to Solitude: The Quest for Privacy in a Crowded World* (Vintage, 1992).

Hammarskjöld, Dag, *Markings* (Faber, 1964).

Hazelden Foundation, *Each Day a New Beginning* (Hazelden Meditation Series, 1982).

Hazrat Inayat Khan, *Gayan Vadan Nirtan* (copyright 1980 Sufi Order, Sufi Order Publications, Lebanon Springs, New York).

Kaye, J. Leonard (ed.)., *The Wisdom of Baltasar Gracián: A Practical Manual for Good and Perilous Times* (Aquarian, 1994).

Koller, Alice, *The Stations of Solitude* (Bantam, 1991).

Kottler, Jeffrey, *Private Moments, Secret Selves: Enriching Our Time Alone* (Jeremy P. Tarcher, Los Angeles, 1990).

Lacont, Pierre, *God is Silence* (Quaker Home Service).

Lavelle, Louis, *Le Mal et La Souffrance* (Libraire Plon, copyright 1940).

Lindbergh, Anne Morrow, *Gifts from the Sea* (Pantheon Books, 1975).

Merton, Thomas, *Thoughts in Solitude* (Burns & Oates, 1958).

Mitchell, Stephen (ed.), *The Enlightened Heart: An Anthology of Sacred Poetry* (HarperCollins).

Muggeridge, Malcolm, *Something Beautiful for God* (Collins).

Nouwen, Henri J. M., *Making All Things New: An Invitation to the Spiritual Life* (Gill & MacMillan, 1982).

Parabola: *Solitude and Community*, vol.xvii, no.1 (1992).

Rinpoche, Sogyal, *Tibetan Book of Living and Dying* (Rider, 1993).

Ross, Maggie, *Seasons of Death and Life: A Wilderness Memoir* (HarperCollins, 1990).

Sarton, May, *Journal of a Solitude: The Intimate Diary of A Year in the Life of a Creative Woman* (Norton, 1977).

Schiff, Francine, *Food for Solitude* (Element Books, 1992).

Storr, Anthony, *Solitude* (Flamingo, 1989).

Thich Nhat Hanh, *Being Peace* (Parallax Press, Berkeley, Ca. 1987).

Thompson, Lewis (ed.)., *Richard Lannoy, Mirror to the Light: Reflections on Consciousness and Experience* (Coventure, 1984).

Thoreau, Henry D., ed. J. Lyndon Stanley, *Walden* (Princetown University Press, 1971).

Trine, Ralph Waldo, *In Tune with the Infinite* (The Aquarian Press, 1991).